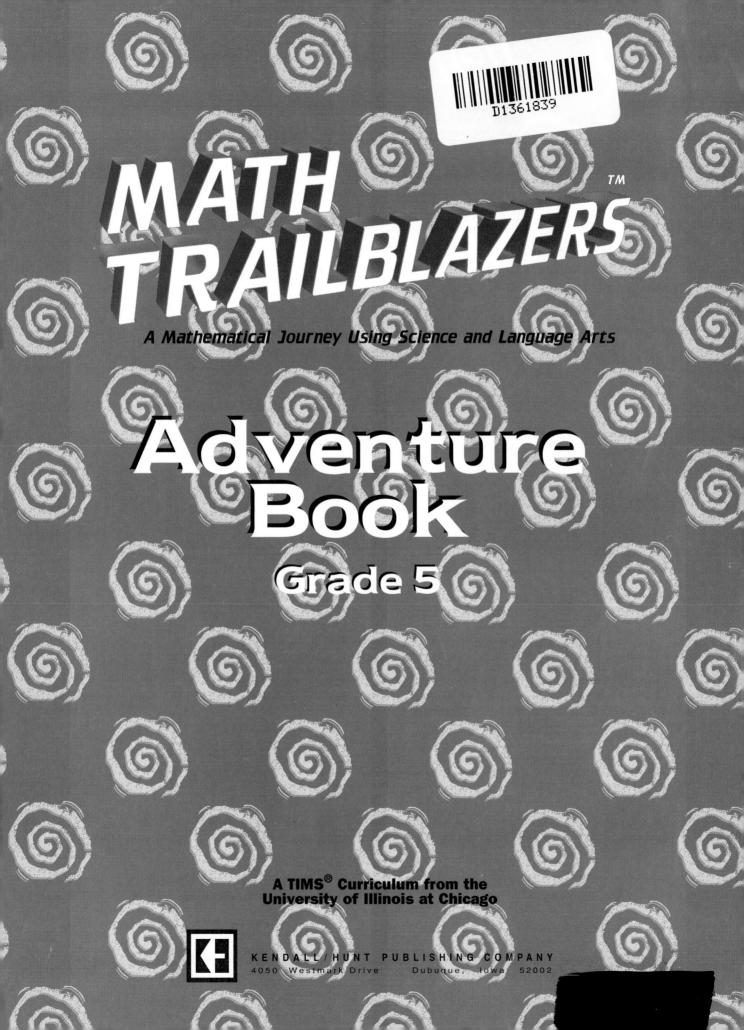

MATH TRAILBLAZERS™

A Mathematical Journey Using Science and Language Arts

Adventure Book
Grade 5

A TIMS® Curriculum from the
University of Illinois at Chicago

KENDALL/HUNT PUBLISHING COMPANY
4050 Westmark Drive   Dubuque, Iowa 52002

MATH TRAILBLAZERS™

Dedication

This book is dedicated to the children and teachers who let us see the magic in their classrooms and to our families who wholeheartedly supported us while we searched for ways to make it happen.

The TIMS Project

Copyright © 1998 by Kendall/Hunt Publishing Company

ISBN 0-7872-0788-8

All rights reserved. No part of this publication may be reproduced, stored in a retrieval system, or transmitted, in any form or by any means, electronic, mechanical, photocopying, recording, or otherwise, without the prior written permission of the copyright owner.

 UIC The University of Illinois at Chicago

This material is based on work supported by the National Science Foundation under grant No. MDR 9050226 and the University of Illinois at Chicago. Any opinions, findings, and conclusions or recommendations expressed in this publication are those of the authors and do not necessarily reflect the views of the granting agencies.

Printed in the United States of America
10 9 8 7 6 5 4 3 2

Table of Contents

Dear Parents,

MATH TRAILBLAZERS™ is based on the belief that all children deserve a challenging mathematics curriculum and that mathematics is best learned through solving many different kinds of problems. The program provides a careful balance of concepts and skills. Traditional arithmetic skills and procedures are covered through their repeated use in problems and through distributed practice.

MATH TRAILBLAZERS™, however, offers much more. Students using this program will become proficient problem solvers, will know how to approach problems in many different ways, will know when and how to apply the mathematics they have learned, and will be able to communicate clearly their mathematical knowledge. They will learn more mathematics than in a traditional program—computation, measurement, geometry, data collection and analysis, estimation, graphing, patterns and relationships, mental arithmetic, and simple algebraic ideas are all an integral part of the curriculum. They will see connections between the mathematics learned in school and the mathematics used in everyday life. And, they will enjoy and value the work they do in mathematics.

This curriculum was built around national recommendations for improving mathematics instruction in American schools and the research that supported those recommendations. It has been extensively tested with thousands of children in dozens of classrooms over five years of development. ***MATH TRAILBLAZERS™*** reflects our view of a complete and well-balanced mathematics program that will prepare children for a world in the 21st century where proficiency in mathematics will be a necessity. We hope that you enjoy this exciting approach to learning mathematics as you watch your child's mathematical abilities grow throughout the year.

Philip Wagreich

Philip Wagreich
Teaching Integrated Mathematics and Science Project
University of Illinois at Chicago
Chicago, Illinois

A Matter of Survival

Betty and her father, Professor Simon Robinson, have been studying monkeys in Brazil's Amazon rain forest. It is early one steamy morning when Betty's mother arrives…

There she is, Dad!

Hello, Alicia!

I have news!

Hi, Mom!

Hello, Professor Robinson.

Hello, Juan.

Gosh! Two Professor Robinsons.

Better call us by our first names.

It's tough having two teachers for parents.

… logging, farming, and raising cattle. Now, we have bare hills and erosion.

The rain forest is the home for at least half of all the different kinds of plants and animals in the world.

Those plants are very important since scientists use them to make many of our medicines.

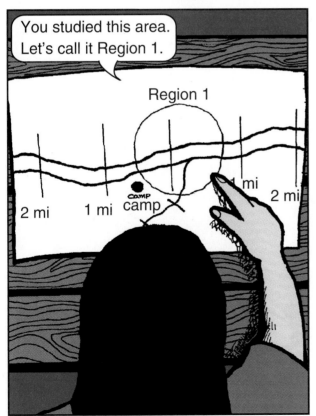

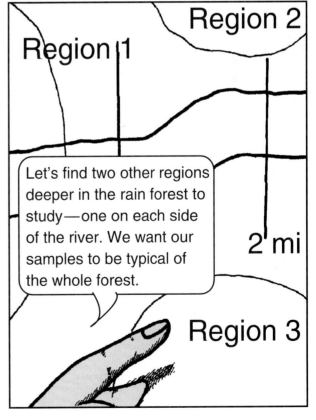

After several days of collecting data, Betty and her father report in.

Here is our data for the spider monkeys, Mom.

T Type of Animal	N Number in Each Region			
	1	2	3	Median
Spider Monkeys	250	210	230	
Squirrels				
River Otters				
Armadillos				
Jaguars				

We'll use the median as an average. Remember, we take the number in the middle.

230 is between 210 and 250. So, the median number of spider monkeys is 230.

Now, the rain forest islands they have been studying in the South have around three times the area of each region we've been studying here.

So, we'd expect 230 times 3—about 690 spider monkeys.

We'll see.

Yes, the rain forest islands should average around 690 spider monkeys if these isolated rain forest "islands" are healthy and provide enough viola plants for the monkeys to eat.

What do we do next?

Sand Reckoning

It's a fine October morning in Oak Park. The sun is shining, but there is a cloud over a certain young Oak Parker: Ellen Novy has to rake the leaves on her front lawn.

"There must be a zillion leaves here, Dad," complained Ellen. "It'll take me forever to rake them all."

"There is no such number as a 'zillion,' Ellen," replied Mr. Novy. "If you work hard I'll bet you can be finished in less than one hour."

"Maybe there's not a zillion leaves here, but there must be at least a billion," said Ellen. "A billion leaves to rake and bag! I'll be old and gray before I'm done. Why don't we recycle the leaves right on the lawn? That'd be more ecological, wouldn't it, Dad?"

"There are certainly fewer than a billion or even a million leaves on that lawn, Ellen. The sooner you get started, the sooner you'll be done."

"How do you know there are fewer than a million leaves, Dad?" asked Ellen.

"Look, our lawn is about 50 feet across and 30 feet from front to back. That's about 1500 square feet. If there were 100 leaves on each square foot—and actually there aren't nearly that many—there would only be 150,000 leaves, which is a lot less than a million. Now, rake!"

Mr. Novy left Ellen to rake. As she raked, she thought about the other girls and boys in her class. Are they playing right now and having a good time? Or are they raking too? Do they have more or fewer leaves to rake? How many leaves need to be raked in Oak Park right now?

Just then, Mrs. Patel, Ellen's neighbor, happened by. "Hello, Ellen," said Mrs. Patel. "Why such a faraway look?"

"Oh, hi, Mrs. Patel," replied Ellen. "I was just wondering how many leaves there are right now on all the lawns in Oak Park. Do you suppose there are more than a trillion?"

"Let's see. A trillion. That's a million millions, right? A 1 followed by twelve 0s. In my work, we call that ten to the twelfth," answered Mrs. Patel. "I'd guess there are far fewer than a trillion, Ellen."

> 1 trillion is 10^{12}.
> Read "ten to the twelfth."
> 1,000,000,000,000

"What about all the leaves on all the lawns in the whole world?" asked Ellen. "Do you think there would be a number big enough for that, Mrs. Patel?"

"Ellen, that question is a lot like a question Archimedes asked long ago."

"Who was Archimedes?" asked Ellen.

"Archimedes," answered Mrs. Patel, "was a mathematician and scientist who lived in Sicily more than two thousand years ago."

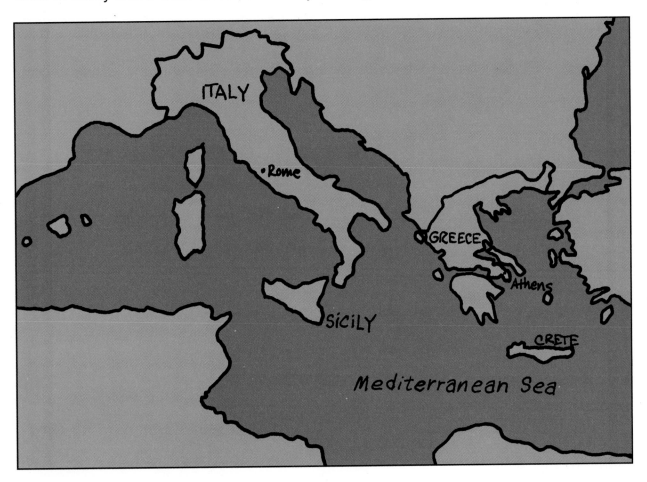

"Where's Sicily?" asked Ellen.

"Sicily is an island in the Mediterranean Sea. If you think of Italy as a boot, then Sicily is right by the toe."

"So what was Archimedes' question that was like mine?" asked Ellen.

"He asked how many grains of sand it would take to fill the whole universe," replied Mrs. Patel.

"My gosh! Imagine filling the whole universe with grains of sand and then counting them! Did he get an answer? Did he really figure out how many grains of sand it would take to fill the whole universe?" asked Ellen.

"Well, Ellen," answered Mrs. Patel, "it's an amazing story. We know about it from a letter Archimedes wrote to King Gelon of Sicily."

"Have you ever eaten a poppy-seed roll, Ellen?" asked Mrs. Patel.

"The kind with the tiny black seeds?" answered Ellen. "Yes, I love them."

"Well, Archimedes got some sand and compared it to a poppy seed. He decided that it would take about 10,000 grains of sand to have the same volume as one poppy seed. Next he compared a poppy seed to a finger-breadth. He decided that about 40 poppy seeds were as wide as a finger."

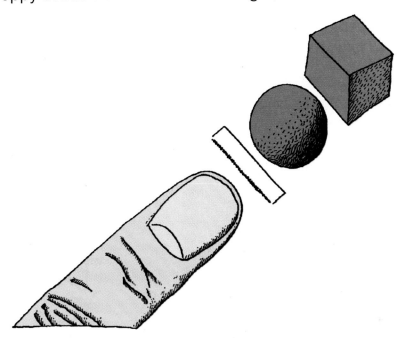

"So Archimedes figured that a sphere with a diameter of one finger-breadth—about the size of a marble—would hold about $40 \times 40 \times 40 = 64,000$ poppy seeds. That meant that about $64,000 \times 10,000 = 640,000,000$ grains of sand would fill a marble-sized sphere. Archimedes worked up and up to larger and larger volumes until he had the number of grains of sand that he thought would fill the whole universe."

"So what number did he finally get for the number of grains of sand to fill the whole universe?" asked Ellen.

"Well," answered Mrs. Patel, "today we would give his answer as 10^{63}— that's a 1 with sixty-three 0s after it."

> 10^{63} is 1,000,000,000,000,000,000,000,000,000,
> 000,000,000,000,000,000,000,000,000,000,000

"Wow! What a monster number!" said Ellen. "Do you think Archimedes was right, Mrs. Patel?"

"Well, Ellen," answered Mrs. Patel, "he did very well for his time, but he underestimated the size of the universe by a good bit. Using a modern idea of the size of the universe, we might get about 10^{90} grains of sand."

> 10^{90} is 1,000,000,000,000,000,000,000,000,000,000,
> 000,000,000,000,000,000,000,000,000,000,
> 000,000,000,000,000,000,000,000,000,000

"That must be the biggest number there is!" said Ellen.

"Not at all, Ellen," replied Mrs. Patel. "There's a number called a googol that is even bigger. A googol is a 1 with one hundred 0s after it, 10^{100}."

> 10^{100} is 10,000,000,000,000,000,000,000,000,000,
> 000,000,000,000,000,000,000,000,000,000,
> 000,000,000,000,000,000,000,000,000,000,
> 000,000,000

"A googol! What a silly name."
"Who thought of that?" asked Ellen.

"The nine-year-old nephew of Dr. Edward Kasner, a mathematician from New York, thought of it."

"It's fun to think about such big numbers," said Ellen. "Is there an even bigger one?"

"There is always a bigger number, Ellen," answered Mrs. Patel. "The biggest I know of that has a name is a googolplex. A googolplex is a 1 with a googol of 0s after it. If we tried to write a googolplex by writing a 1 and putting a googol of 0s after it, we'd need a piece of paper that would stretch past the farthest star. But even though a googolplex is a huge number, there are still others bigger."

"You mean the numbers keep going on and on forever and ever?" asked Ellen.

"That's right," answered Mrs. Patel.

Just then, Ellen's father arrived to see how the raking was coming along.

"Hello, Mrs. Patel," said Mr. Novy. "How's your work at the lab coming?"

"Very well, thank you. We have been getting some very interesting measurements lately," answered Mrs. Patel. "You know, Ellen might make a fine scientist someday. She and I were just having a discussion about very large numbers."

"Yeah, Dad," said Ellen. "Did you know that numbers go on forever and ever? Did you ever hear of a googol or a googolplex? How many grains of sand do you think it would take to fill the whole universe?"

"Grains of sand in the universe?" asked Mr. Novy. "A gogool-*what*? On and on *forever*? That's how long it will take you to rake these leaves at the rate you're going. Are you hoping they will rake themselves?"

"That's a great idea, Dad, self-raking leaves," answered Ellen. "But no, this won't take forever. There's just about no leaves here at all, compared to a googol. I'll finish in no time. Then will you take me to the library? I want to get a book about Archimedes."

George Washington Carver: Man of Measure

"And Honorable Mention goes to Yucca and Cactus, painted by George Washington Carver!"

In 1893, at the World's Columbian Exposition in Chicago, a young artist named George Washington Carver watched in amazement and joy as his painting of a beautiful flowering cactus received an award. "Perhaps my dream of having a career as a painter will come true after all," he thought.

At that time, Carver was a college student, studying plants, at Iowa State University. However, many of his friends and teachers believed that he would eventually become a great artist. Carver himself had long felt that he had a special gift, but he knew that painting was only one of the many talents he possessed. Now he longed to feel certain about his life's work; he felt strongly that it was time for him to choose a path and follow it. But he was not so sure that painting was the path he was meant to follow.

George roamed among the exhibits at the fair, eagerly exploring the latest discoveries that science and technology had to offer. He was amazed by the acres of fine buildings, and he stared in wonder at telescopes, steam engines, printing presses, and much more.

However, it was to the horticulture and agriculture buildings he kept returning, spending hours fascinated by their displays. Even as a student in Iowa, George was highly respected for his impressive knowledge of how plants grew and his research in the field of mycology (study of fungi).

In Chicago, he examined strange and wonderful new tools for farming; he saw fantastic varieties of seeds; and he was amazed by the possibilities offered by the new science of genetics. Everything he saw in these buildings reminded him that scientific agriculture could mean better lives for all farmers.

Carver looked around at the people in the vast hall. Almost all of them were white. In 1893, Black people were not often allowed to mix with white people. Carver had been admitted to the hall in order to show his painting, but other African Americans could visit the hall only on special days. He felt very much alone and longed to help his people.

"The poor Black farmers I grew up with in the South could benefit from so many of the ideas in these exhibits, if they were only given the opportunity," Carver thought.

Carver knew from his childhood in the South that there were many poor, Black people struggling to survive in the years after the end of slavery. There were not many jobs. Some lived as farmers who rented land and tried to scratch a living from the soil. Others had moved north to big cities like Chicago to find work. But the jobs available to them were low-paying and offered little chance for advancement or security.

During Carver's trip to the World's Columbian Exposition, he was alarmed by the poverty and helplessness he saw in Chicago's ghettoes. He believed that even with its harsh conditions, the rural South offered more opportunities for his people than the urban centers of the North.

"I could become a painter—but how much would that help my people?" Carver wondered. He was troubled by the problems faced by so many of his people, and his deepest wish was to be of service to them. Now, with all the wonders of agricultural science before him, he knew which career he should select. He could best serve his race by teaching them to farm. He would use the power of scientific agriculture to help his people—and all people.

Three years later in 1896, as a new teacher at Tuskeegee Institute in Alabama, Carver was ready to explode with frustration. He wondered how he could possibly teach science without having a laboratory. He took his problem to the principal of the Institute, Booker T. Washington.

"Mr. Principal, this is impossible!" Carver exclaimed. "Even the school cook has better equipment than I do!"

Washington was sympathetic but firm. "Calm down, Mr. Carver," he said. "Of course you need more equipment for your laboratory, but you know how little money we have right now."

Carver was at a loss. There was never an answer for the lack of money. He begged Booker T. Washington to help him figure out what to do. Washington sighed. "That, I'm afraid, is a very difficult problem," he replied. "There is so much to be done here—you know that everyone is overworked. I don't doubt your ability or your dedication, Mr. Carver. What I ask is that you continue to do all that you can to help our people using the limited resources we have available."

"Forgive me, Mr. Washington," Carver interrupted, "but I require a better lab so that I can conduct scientific research. I want to find ways to grow better crops and determine which garden vegetables are the most nutritious. To do this, I must test the plants and the soils."

"Trust me," replied Washington, "As soon as we have the funds, I will see to it that you get more equipment. You'll have the best science laboratory in the South. Meanwhile, do the best you can with what you have—and be patient."

But Carver was not patient. He decided to ask his students to help him equip a lab in a way the Institute could afford.

The next day, Carver spoke to his students. "We need more containers for measuring and storing materials in our lab. Do any of you know where we can find some old jars or cans?"

"There's a dump full of trash behind the barns near here. Sometimes we find interesting things there," said Lydell.

"Excellent!" Carver replied. "Let's go and have a look!"

At the dump, another student, Andrew, watched his teacher and classmates poking through the piles of garbage. "But Professor Carver—you don't mean to use waste from the dump in our lab, do you?"

"I certainly do, Andrew!" said Carver. "As a matter of fact, I don't believe there should be such a thing as waste. Look around you! Do you see Nature producing any waste? Waste is what people make when we fail to apply our intelligence to find creative uses for waste products."

"But why do we need containers for measuring?" asked Andrew. "We have the ones you brought with you from Iowa."

"Well, Andrew, for our laboratory, we will need enough equipment including containers so that each student can accurately measure the variables you will be investigating in your experiments."

Suddenly Carver saw something and cried out, "Aha! Look what I found!"

Andrew looked at his teacher's find doubtfully, "That's just a tangled mess of old string. It's not good for anything."

Carver smiled and put the string in his pocket. "We'll see."

Then Carver picked up a bent pie plate and a teacup with a broken handle. "Perfect! Exactly what we need!"

"Need for what, Professor Carver?" asked James. "What are they?"

"James, this pie plate should make a good specimen dish, and I think this teacup will make a fine beaker," answered Carver.

"If you say so, sir," James replied.

Carver turned around. "Say, look sharp there, Herschel! You're just about to step on a graduated cylinder!"

"You mean this skinny old jar?" asked Herschel.

"Yes, I do, Herschel. Wrap it in a rag and put it on the cart of supplies we'll take back to the lab."

An hour later, Carver said, "It looks like the cart's just about full—let's go back to the classroom. Tomorrow, we will start turning these things into equipment we can use in our lab."

The next day in the classroom, with the pile of odd containers from the dump spread on a table, the students gathered around their teacher. Carver began, "Yesterday, Andrew asked why we need containers for measuring. Measuring variables is an important part of science. For instance, when scientists do experiments, they often need to measure variables such as length, area, volume, mass, and time."

"What do you mean by measuring a variable?" asked Herschel.

Carver thought for a moment and then replied, "Let's think about the five fundamental variables that I just named and how we measure them. We can start with time. What do we use to measure time, and what are its standard units?"

Herschel answered, "We measure time with a clock. Minutes are the units."

"Very good—but are there other standard units for time besides minutes?"

"Sure," answered Herschel. "There are seconds, hours, days, months . . ."

Carver noticed a hand waving in the back of the room. "Lydell, do you have a question?"

"Yes, sir. What's a standard unit, anyway?"

"Can anyone answer Lydell's question?"

"Well," offered James, "Is it like a tool for finding out how much of something there is?"

"In a way, yes," said Carver. "Take length as an example: What if we wanted to know how long this table is? What would we need in order to measure its length?"

"We could use your yardstick," suggested Andrew.

"And what are the standard units on the yardstick?" Carver asked.

Herschel answered, "The yardstick is divided into inches. Each one of them is exactly the same length."

"Right—and that's why we call an inch a standard unit of length," said Carver.

"So," added James, "Since we need yardsticks for our lab, we can make more. We could cut strips of wood the same size as your yardstick and then use your yardstick to mark off inches on the new one."

"Great, James—we'll do that! You've got the right idea. We start with what we know—in this case, inches—and use them to make more yardsticks. Now let's think about measuring area. Can someone tell me exactly what area is?"

"Area is length times width," Herschel declared.

"Good try, Herschel, but length times width is actually a formula for measuring the area of a rectangle. Can someone explain the idea of area in words that aren't a formula?"

James raised his hand. "Isn't area the amount of surface it takes to cover something?"

"Excellent, James. Can you also tell me what are the standard units for measuring area?"

"That depends on what you're measuring," James replied. "We would use acres to measure a farm, but we would use other units to measure other things. For example, this table could be measured in square inches."

"And how would you measure the area of this table?" asked Carver.

"Like I said!" Herschel reminded the class. "It's the length in inches times the width in inches."

Carver laughed. "This time that's exactly right, Herschel. Now something else we need for the lab is a set of containers for measuring volume, which is the amount of space occupied by an object. Let's begin by making a container that will hold exactly 1 liter. How should we start?"

James answered in the way he thought his teacher would answer the question himself: "I think we should start with what we know."

"And what might that be?" asked Carver with a smile.

"Uh . . . I'm not sure," James admitted sheepishly.

Carver pointed to the shelf behind him. "Why don't you look up here and see if you can find something that measures volume?"

"How about that skinny bottle with the lines on it?" asked James.

Carver took the graduated cylinder from the shelf. "Good—we can use this container for measuring volume. When we fill it up to the top line, it holds exactly 100 milliliters. So we call it a 100-milliliter graduated cylinder. Now can someone tell me how we can use this to make a 1-liter container?"

Herschel raised his hand. "Aren't there 1000 milliliters in one liter?"

Carver nodded. "That's right."

"So," Herschel said, "if we fill the graduated cylinder ten times and put all the water into one jar, we will have one liter, and then we can mark the level of 1 liter of water on the jar."

A few minutes later, Herschel proudly addressed his teacher. "We're finished, Professor Carver—here's our first 1-liter container!"

"Fine!" Carver answered. "We've gotten a good start on making standards for length, area, and volume. Now who has an idea about how to make standards to measure mass, which is the amount of matter in an object?"

James stood up. "I see something we could use to make a set of standard masses. Couldn't we use these little cans and fill them up with sand until they have the same mass as the standard ones?"

"That should work well," Carver said.

"But how can we know when they're the right mass?" Lydell asked.

"Look at what I've made, Lydell," directed Carver.

He reached into a cabinet and lifted out a balance made from pieces of wood, tin plates, and the untangled string. "With the materials we gathered from the dump and a clear understanding of how to measure mass, we can build enough balances for the whole class. We can use the balances to measure mass."

Through an understanding of science and measurement, Carver and his students were able to equip their first lab with the materials available to them. From this meager beginning, George Washington Carver went on to establish one of the most significant agricultural experimental stations of the twentieth century.

Unlikely Heroes

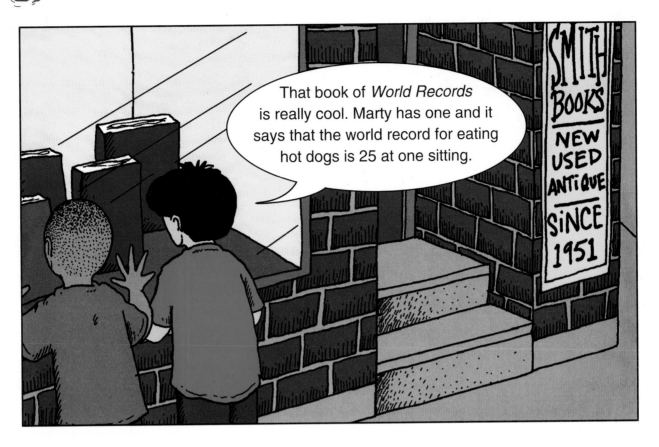

Early in World War II, Nazi armies under Adolf Hitler conquered most of Europe.

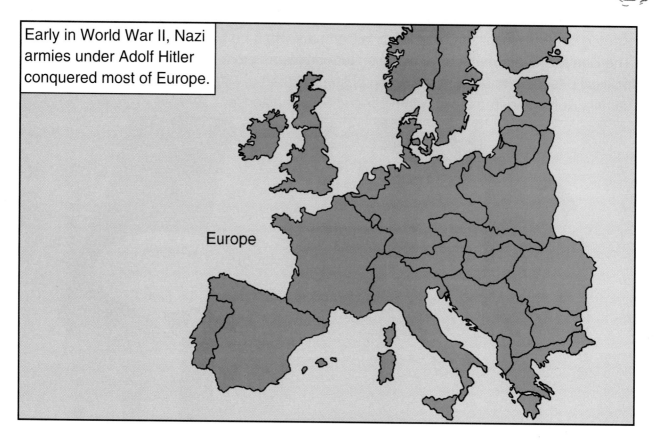

Europe

Many people were imprisoned by the Nazis for their political beliefs or because of their race or nationality.

Kerrich, an English citizen, was living in Denmark when he was arrested. The Danish government convinced the German leaders to allow Danish political prisoners to be sent to Danish prisons instead of Nazi concentration camps. Kerrich shared a cell with his friend Eric Christensen.

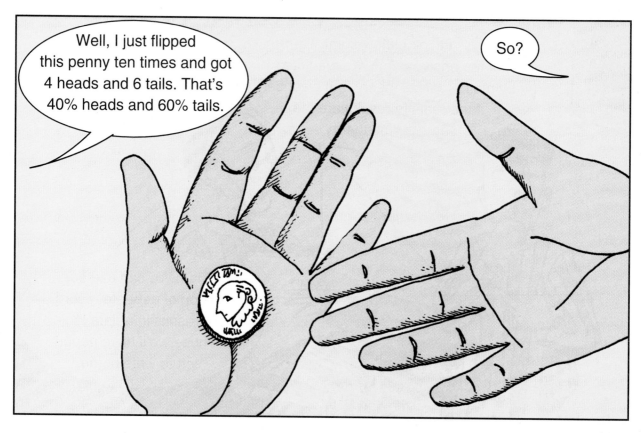

TTTHH	HTHTT	HHHHH	THTTT
HHTHT	HHHHT	TTHTT	HHHTT
HTTTT	THHHT	TTHTH	THTHT
THTTT	THTTH	HTTTH	TTTTH
HHTHT	HTTTH	TTTTH	THHTH
THHHT	HTTTT	HHTHT	THTHT
TTTTH	HHHHT	HHHHH	TTHHT
HHTTH	THTHH	THTHT	TTTTH
HTTTH	HHTTH	HHHHT	HHTHT
HTHHT	HTTHH	THHTH	HTHHT
THHHH	HTTTT	HHHTH	HTTTH
THTTH	TTTTT	HTHTT	HHHHH
HTHHH	THTHH	HTTTH	HTTTH
HTTTH	HTTTH	HTTHH	THTTH
TTTTH	TTTTH	HHTHH	HHTTT
HHHHH	HHTTT	TTTTT	THHTH
THHTH	TTHHH	HHTHH	HHTTH
TTHTH	THHTT	HHHTH	HTHHH
TTHTT	TTTHT	TTHHT	THTHH
TTHHH	HHTHT	THHHH	TTTHT

Kerrich and Christensen could see that in only a few flips, there might not be the same number of heads and tails. But they predicted that in a large number of flips, the number of heads and tails would be about the same. They continued their experiment until they reached 10,000 flips. They organized their data in a data table like this one:

Number of Flips	Number of Heads	Number of Tails	Percent Heads	Percent Tails		Number of Flips	Number of Heads	Number of Tails	Percent Heads	Percent Tails
1	0	1	0%	100%		200	98	102	49%	51%
2	0	2	0%	100%		300	146	154	49%	51%
3	0	3	0%	100%		400	199	201	50%	50%
4	1	3	25%	75%		500	255	245	51%	49%
5	2	3	40%	60%		600	312	288	52%	48%
6	3	3	50%	50%		700	368	332	53%	47%
7	3	4	43%	57%		800	413	387	52%	48%
8	4	4	50%	50%		900	458	442	51%	49%
9	4	5	44%	56%		1000	502	498	50%	50%
10	4	6	40%	60%		2000	1013	987	51%	49%
20	10	10	50%	50%		3000	1510	1490	50%	50%
30	17	13	57%	43%		4000	2029	1971	51%	49%
40	21	19	52%	48%		5000	2533	2467	51%	49%
50	25	25	50%	50%		6000	3009	2991	50%	50%
60	29	31	48%	52%		7000	3516	3484	50%	50%
70	32	38	46%	54%		8000	4034	3966	50%	50%
80	35	45	44%	56%		9000	4538	4462	50%	50%
90	40	50	44%	56%		10,000	5067	4933	51%	49%
100	44	56	44%	56%						

When Kerrich graphed the data for 10, 100, and 10,000 flips, he was able to see more clearly the relationship between the heads and the tails.

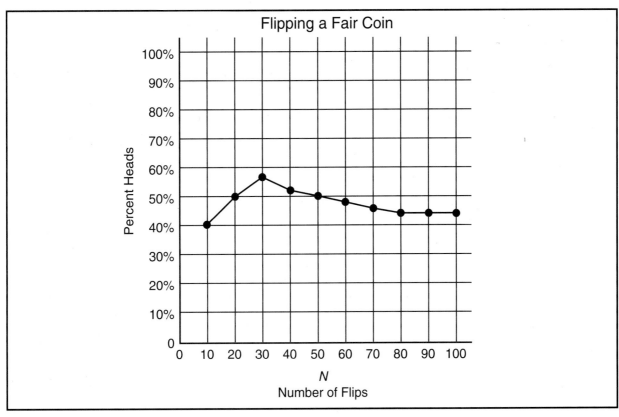

Kerrich continued his work by doing other experiments. In one experiment, he attached lead to one side of the coin. He wondered if making one side of the coin heavier than the other would make the coin unfair.

This graph shows the results.

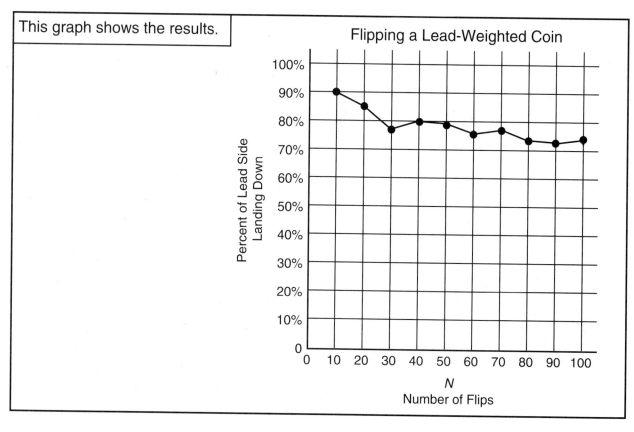

Flipping a Lead-Weighted Coin

Percent of Lead Side Landing Down

N
Number of Flips

After the war, Kerrich published a book about his experiments, *An Experimental Introduction to the Theory of Probability.* He and Christensen were remarkable men, not only for the valuable work they did while Danish prisoners, but for their determination to make the best of an unfortunate ordeal.

Gee, I guess that flipping a coin over and over was not a waste of time after all. Let's go flip this quarter and see what happens.

Maybe we can try that later. Now I'm going to try to beat the hot dog record. I'm going across the street to eat 26 hot dogs!

Florence Kelley

In the late 19th century, many immigrant families were forced to send their children to work. The mothers and fathers could not earn enough money to take care of the family. Employers often hired children because they did not have to pay them as much as they would pay a grownup. Our story, a true incident, begins on Christmas Eve, 1892, in a poor Chicago neighborhood.

"Papa!" Ten-year-old Antonio rushed to greet his father, who stood at the front door shaking the snow out of his boots. His mother spoke to her husband in a worried tone, "I'm so glad you are here—Frannie hasn't come home yet! We've heard nothing since she left at six o'clock this morning."

Papa stopped taking off his coat. "But it's almost one o'clock in the morning! Where is she? Did she find work?"

"I don't know," Mama explained. "One of the candy stores was hiring girls, so she set out this morning to see if she could get a job."

Papa bent over to pull his boots on again. "I'm going to look for her!"

Mama put a hand on his arm. "But we have no idea which candy store she went to! She's only 13—it frightens me to think of her out on the streets all alone." Just then the door flew open and Francesca stumbled in.

Antonio darted forward. "Frannie, where were you? We were so scared!" Her mother took her by the hands. "Bambina mia, you're so cold! Come, tell us what happened."

After Francesca caught her breath, she began to speak. "Well, this morning I set out for the candy shop. It turned out to be several miles away. But I was lucky! I was the oldest of all the girls waiting there, and because I was able to speak a little English, I was chosen for the job. It was a terribly long day. I worked straight through until midnight, stopping only to eat the apple Mama gave me this morning—but I dared not complain. At midnight, the boss gave me 50 cents and told me the job was finished. They had only wanted me for one day."

"When I went outside, the streetcars had stopped running, so I had to walk home. Papa, I was so frightened! It was cold and dark, and there were men on the street who spoke to me. I walked quickly and kept my eyes ahead of me. When I was close to home, I ran as fast as I could!"

Mama hugged her daughter. "Poor darling—I'm so glad you're safe!"

Antonio suddenly remembered. "It's Christmas morning! Buon Natale! Can we open our presents?"

Everyone looked at Papa and waited. He smiled. "You're right, Antonio," he said. "It's Christmas—and we have much to celebrate. What do you say, Mama? Shall we have our Christmas cake and some tea?"

"Yes, let's," agreed Mama. She went to the cupboard and took out two small packages. "I'm afraid there's not much," she apologized.

Antonio eagerly tore open his present. "Oh, boy! A whistle and a top! Grazie, Papa! Grazie, Mama!"

Francesca unwrapped her present and looked at it in puzzlement. "A book?" she asked. "In English? But I can't read English!"

Papa laughed and explained, "There is a settlement house in our neighborhood where we can learn English. It's called Hull House. It is run by a lady named Jane Addams. She and the other women who live there offer all kinds of classes and clubs. And the classes won't cost anything."

Mama added, "They are held in the evenings, so Antonio and you can go even if you have to work during the day. I know it will be hard, after working all day. But if you can learn English well, there will be so many more opportunities for you."

Francesca threw her arms around her parents. "Mille grazie!" she cried, and then quickly added in English, "I mean, thank you very much!"

That spring, one evening after working all day, Francesca and Antonio were sitting in a Hull House English class. A large, rather fierce-looking lady was writing the name "Florence Kelley" on the chalkboard. The lady turned to the class, looking out from under huge black braids that were wrapped around her head. The young students nervously glanced at each other. They dared not make a sound. They expected this woman to bellow commands at them and worried that they would not understand. When Florence Kelley smiled kindly at them and spoke in gentle tones, the entire class seemed to relax.

Florence Kelley was new to Hull House. She had arrived in Chicago only a few months before. Like all the women who lived and worked at Hull House, she did much more than teach. Kelley had spent all of her adult life working to improve conditions for the poor. She had made a special study of the lives of poor children who were forced to work long hours in factories or sweatshops, and she was determined to work for laws that would make child labor illegal.

Now Florence Kelley concentrated on the task before her. She knew the importance of teaching these children to speak and read English. She knew that children who could not speak English would have little choice about the kinds of work they could do.

"And who can read these words?" she asked, pointing to the chalkboard. Antonio tried to pay attention, but he was so tired after working all day. The words began to blur in front of his eyes. The teacher turned to look at the class just as Antonio's head slumped forward onto the table. "Oh, my—" she said. "Is that poor boy sleeping?"

Francesca shook her brother and explained, "Antonio has a new job at the tin-can factory. He worked ten hours today."

Antonio felt his face turn red. "I'm sorry, Miss. I'm awake now."

Kelley patted his arm. "Don't worry, Antonio. But tell me—what is this job of yours at the factory?"

"I'm a shelf-boy," Antonio explained. "I sit on a small platform in between the floors of the factory. We push pieces of tin through little slits in the platform, and they fall into containers below." He held up a bandaged hand. "Sometimes we get cut."

Kelley could barely contain her fury. She had heard this story too many times before about children working and getting hurt on the job. "But this is madness! How many of the rest of you have worked today?" Kelley asked. Nine of the students raised their hands. "And how many of you are over 16 years old?" Only one raised her hand.

There was bitterness in Kelley's voice as she vented her anger. "It is terrible that so many of you are forced to spend your days in such a way. There ought to be laws against it! For now, however, we shall hurry to finish this lesson so you can go home and get some rest."

Later that night Florence Kelley was sitting in her tiny room, looking at the papers the children had written in class. Hearing a soft knock, she rose to find Jane Addams at the door. "Florence, may I interrupt you for a moment?"

"Of course, Miss Addams! Please come in."

Addams sat down. "I see you are grading English papers," she said. "How is the class going?"

"Not badly," answered Kelley. "The children are delightful—very bright and eager to learn. The trouble is that many of them are very tired from working long hours at their jobs during the day. When I think of it, I get so angry I could spit nails!"

Jane Addams smiled calmly at her spirited friend. "Ah, then you will be very interested in this letter from the Illinois Bureau of Labor Statistics. They would like you to write a report on the sweatshops of Chicago."

Kelley was immediately interested. "What exactly do they want?" she asked, as she skimmed through the letter.

"It is a huge task," admitted Addams. "They want you to make at least 1000 visits in the neighborhood—go to shops, factories, businesses, and homes and ask the people a long list of questions. That way, the government will be able to gather precise data on what living conditions are like for the poor."

Kelley jumped up and began to pace the room. "Yes! This is the kind of research I've been saying should be done! By collecting actual numbers, and by doing it again in future years, we will be able to show whether things are getting better or worse. This is exactly the kind of data that agencies need if they are to plan effective programs to help the poor! Investigating the sweatshops will provide real data to convince the public and the lawmakers that child labor is a real problem."

Addams was not surprised at Kelley's enthusiasm. "I knew you would see the importance of this survey. That was why I recommended you for the job."

"Oh, thank you, Miss Addams!" Kelley exclaimed. "I can't wait to get started!"

In the years that followed, Florence Kelley continued to gather data. Her surveys included factories and households as well as the sweatshops. She and her

assistants spent many long days trudging the streets of Chicago. They knocked on doors, wrote down what they saw, and asked people questions.

They saw homes that were neat and clean and homes that were bare and dirty. Some apartments had no windows. The air inside smelled of coal stoves and cooking grease. Many had no running water or toilets. Some of the factories were even worse, with their loud and dangerous machines. Some people even lived in the same rooms in which they operated small businesses or factories. Here children as young as three years old could be found hard at work beside their parents. Even toddlers could pull the basting threads out of clothing that had been stitched by their mothers.

Kelley and her workers talked to hundreds of people and asked many questions. They asked how many children were in each family and where the people worked. They found out how much money each family earned and what languages they spoke. They learned where people had been born and whether they could read and write. They took careful notes and kept a record of every answer.

In the course of her investigations, Florence Kelley was able to prove that great numbers of children were working instead of going to school. These children were poor and uneducated and often worked long hours in terrible conditions. By using her survey data to support her arguments, she convinced many more people that there was a serious problem and that something should be done about it.

However, Kelley did not believe that the United States government in Washington, D.C., would be able to change this anytime soon. She decided to ask the Illinois state legislators to investigate for themselves, in the hope that they would pass state laws against child labor. She wrote reports and made speeches. She even took the lawmakers on tours of the worst factories to show them firsthand what children were being exposed to.

In the summer of 1893, Illinois passed its first factory law. The law made it illegal for children to work more than eight hours a day and illegal for children under the age of fourteen to work at all. There was also a requirement that factories be inspected, to make sure they were obeying the new law. Florence Kelley was appointed the first Chief Inspector of Factories in Illinois, a job she energetically carried out for four years.

Four years later:

Each year that she worked as Chief Factory Inspector, Florence Kelley wrote a long report to the governor. It included all the facts she had collected in that year. One day soon after the publication of her Third Annual Report, she strode into Jane Addams's office without even knocking.

"Dearest Miss Addams,—I've been looking over some of the survey data for the last few years—just take a look at the numbers in the 'Increase in Work Done' data table! Look at the numbers of children who are employed."

Addams had long become used to Kelley's ways and did not seem to mind the interruption. She cast her eye down the page of tables that Kelley was holding out to her. "Hmmm," she said, not quite understanding. "But it looks to me as though there are more children employed now than there were last year."

Third Annual Report
of the
Factory Inspectors of Illinois

Increase in Work Done.

Year	Places inspected.	Men employed.	Women employed.	Children employed.	Total employed.
1895.........................	4,540	151,075	30,670	8,624	190,369
1894.........................	3,440	97,600	24,335	8,130	130,065
Increase................	1,100	53,475	6,335	494	60,304
1895.........................	4,540	151,075	30,670	8,624	190,369
1893.........................	2,362	52,480	17,288	6,456	76,224
Increase................	2,178	98,595	13,382	2,168	114,145

"Yes, but look more closely. Look at the numbers of factories inspected and the number of children employed." Kelley was triumphant.

Addams looked up and smiled. "That's wonderful, Florence!"

But Kelley was not finished. "I think these numbers show a trend," she declared, "a trend toward a reduction in the number of children employed. And I predict because of the new law that this trend will continue—these yearly Factory Inspector's reports seem to be making an impact. Why, we can see the difference right here in our own neighborhood! Only yesterday, Francesca told me that she and Antonio could find fewer and fewer employers willing to hire them. Their parents have decided that they may as well go to school!"

Jane Addams was happy to agree. "I am sure you are right," she said. "By exposing what the factories and sweatshops are doing, you have gotten the public on our side. Businessmen respect the power of public opinion. To keep their customers, they have to listen and make changes."

Florence Kelley fairly twinkled with glee. She banged her fist happily on Jane Addams's desk, making her jump. "I can't wait to see next year's figures! If this trend continues, it will prove that new laws and careful research can bring about changes in society."

Wherefore Art Thou, Romeo?

At the Ridgewood School, getting ready for a group of visiting actors.

No, sir.

You ever work lights before, kid?

Well, it's easy. What's your name, kid?

Howard, sir.

The principal introduces the first scene.

Hello, children. First, we will see the famous scene from Shakespeare's *Hamlet.*

Hamlet thinks his father the king has been murdered, but he is not positive and also not sure what to do or say… *To be or not to be…*

HOLD IT! The actor will do that! Gosh, what a ham!

The houselights dim. Hamlet finds his mark. It's dark. Howard types in…

Let's see… ordered pair $x = 3$ m, $y = -5$ m. Oh no! Is that (-5 m, +3 m)? I'll try (-5 m, 3 m).

And out of the dark comes the spotlight.

To be or not to be!

Rincker Memorial Library-Concordia

Romeo tries to reach the spotlight, but...

OUCH!

BONK!

The tree crashes into the balcony as the houselights come up.

HELP!

CRASH!

Peanut Soup

A Story About George Washington Carver and His Students

Many years after his arrival at Tuskegee Institute, George Washington Carver was still experimenting, teaching, and trying to convince the poorest farmers that they could make a good life for themselves and their families in the rural South.

One day, Carver's students found their teacher with his head in his hands. They waited quietly by the door. Louis broke the silence. "Excuse me, Professor—would it be better if we came back later for class?"

Carver looked up and rose to greet them. "No, no—come in, Louis. All of you, please come in! I'm sorry I've been so preoccupied lately. I've had a lot on my mind."

"You've been cooped up here in the lab for days," said Alberta. "We were getting worried about you."

"Thank you, Alberta. I appreciate your concern. But let me explain what I've been doing."

Carver pointed to his lab table, which was covered with vials, pans, and bottles. "Everything you see here—this shoe polish, this face cream, even this glass of milk—I made from peanuts. The possibilities are endless! There's shaving cream, house paint—and look at this! I think this would make excellent linoleum! I made it from peanut shells."

"You made all this from *goobers?*" asked Eugene. "All this stuff?"

Before Carver could answer, young Buford, the smallest of the group, asked, "Why did you want to make stuff out of goobers?"

Carver gestured toward the window and the farmland beyond. "Well, Buford, it's because I made a promise to the farmers around here, and they've been asking me when I'm going to keep it."

"A promise?" Louis asked.

"That's right," explained Carver. "I've been telling the farmers to plant peanuts instead of growing cotton. Our work here at Tuskegee has shown that peanuts are good for the soil and the crops they grow now are ruining the soil. You see, cotton takes nitrogen from the soil, and nitrogen must be present for most plants to grow. Peanuts and other legumes like cowpeas and soybeans put nitrogen back into the soil by 'fixing' it so that the plants can use it."

While Carver spoke, Eugene and Buford studied the items on the lab table. "Is there anything good to eat here?" Buford asked. "Sure, Buford," replied a skeptical Eugene, "Why don't you take a bite of that linoleum and tell me what you think!"

Alberta reminded Carver that he hadn't yet explained what his promise to the farmers had been.

"I promised that they would be able to make a profit by selling their peanuts," Carver said. "I told them that there would be a good market for their crops. Trouble is, I was the only one who could imagine the value of the peanut. But now, I have found dozens of ways for peanuts to be used!"

"Wow, Professor," exclaimed Louis, "I can hardly believe you made all of these things from goobers! Could I try the shoe polish?"

"Yes—try anything you like. And let me know what you think."

"This face cream is wonderful!" said Alberta. "Now will you show the farmers how to make all these things?"

"I'm afraid it's not that simple, Alberta," Carver replied. "Farmers don't have the time or the equipment to make all these things for themselves. It wouldn't be efficient. What the farmers need is for someone to buy their peanuts. They need businessmen to open factories to make peanut products. Unfortunately, the businessmen around here don't think very highly of our lowly goober. I could show these products to local businessmen, and they would listen politely, but they would probably still think that goobers are only good for hog feed and fertilizer. I wish there were some way I could get them to 'catch the vision' and see all the economic potential that is locked up in a little peanut."

Buford had been waiting for a chance to be heard. "But, Professor, I don't see anything to eat here! The thing I like best about goobers is eating them. Why, all the folks I know like to eat goobers—doesn't everybody?"

Eugene was doubtful. "I don't think so, Buford—I know Black folks eat goobers, but I've never seen any white folks eating them."

"Hey, Professor—this is giving me an idea!" exclaimed Louis. "Maybe if we show those businessmen just how good goobers are to eat, they might be more willing to invest their money."

"You know, Louis, that's not a bad idea. What exactly did you have in mind?"

"Well, I think we should start by convincing their stomachs. We could prepare a delicious meal for them with all our favorite goober dishes."

Buford piped up, "Well, I wish they could eat some of my Ma's goober cookies. Then they would see how good goobers are."

Louis nodded. "And my Momma makes the best goober soup you ever ate—we eat it all the time!"

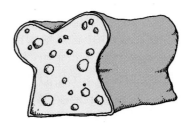

"My auntie works in the kitchens here at Tuskegee," added Alberta, "and she brings us the leftover goober bread."

Carver was enthusiastic. "I have been collecting goober—I mean peanut—recipes for some time now. If you all bring in your favorite recipes, we could experiment to find out which ones taste the best, and then use those. And, by the way, we really ought to start calling the goober by its correct common name, the peanut."

"Okay," agreed Louis. "And who knows? Maybe people who think goobers are hog food might not feel so bad about eating peanuts!"

The next week, Carver and his class gathered in the kitchen of Tuskegee's guest house. "All right, class, let's get down to business. I have an announcement to make. Twelve members of the Macon County Businessmen's Association have accepted our luncheon invitation. They'll be coming here two weeks from Saturday. Our experiments with recipes have been going well, but now we need to finish up and decide on the final menu. I would like you to work in groups today with each group in charge of one recipe."

"I brought my aunt's bread recipe," Alberta said. "I could take that one."

"That's fine, Alberta. Josephine can take charge of her soup recipe. I'll work on the peanut and sweet potato loaf I call mock chicken."

Alberta turned to Eugene. "Right! For the bread, first we'll need flour—Eugene, would you please fetch the flour we need from the pantry?"

Eugene looked at the recipe and said, "Yes, but, Miss Alberta, this recipe says—"

Alberta interrupted. "Please, just read the recipe and fetch the right amount of flour!"

Eugene picked up an enormous metal bowl and headed for the pantry. "If you say so."

Alberta addressed two of her fellow students, "While Eugene's getting the flour, we can look for the right-size pans."

Eugene returned from the pantry with a huge bowl of flour. "Here you go, Alberta. This is the first batch—I figure I'll have to fetch about ten more bowls to have enough."

Alberta stared down at him. "What are you thinking? There is enough flour here for two banquets!"

"No, ma'am," Eugene replied. "That recipe says plain as day that we need 70 pounds of flour for the bread."

Alberta took up the recipe. "Let me see that."

She read the instructions. "Well, no wonder! This recipe makes enough bread to feed half the students at Tuskegee! We'll have to make much less than this recipe says to make."

"That's a good idea," joked Eugene. "Maybe if we cut it down far enough, those businessmen won't even notice the peanuts in it."

"Don't be silly, Eugene. The amount of peanuts—I mean the ratio—of peanuts to bread will stay the same."

"Ratio?" asked Eugene.

"Relax," replied Alberta. "A ratio is just a fraction. We can use fractions to solve our flour problem."

"How?"

"Let's follow the Professor's advice and start with what we know. Look at your bread recipe and tell me how many people it serves."

Eugene looked at the recipe. "This says, 'Feeds 240.' "

"But we'll only have 12 men at the luncheon," Alberta pointed out.

"Yeah—so the recipe you gave me is way too big."

"Right! So can you tell me how much flour you'll need for our bread?"

"Let's see . . ." Eugene thought. "I think I can. If we divide 240 people by 12 people, we get 20. This means the recipe makes 20 times more than we need. So we should divide each ingredient by 20."

"Good thinking, Eugene! You're right. You do know how to use ratios!"

Eugene was puzzled. "Ratios? When did I use a ratio?"

Alberta patiently wrote out the ratio she had in mind:

$$\frac{\text{people served at luncheon}}{\text{people served with recipe}} = \frac{12 \text{ people}}{240 \text{ people}}$$

Eugene easily saw what Alberta was trying to say. "So ratios are like fractions," he said. "But wait a minute! That's not the way I did it. I divided 240 by 12. What you have is just the opposite. You are dividing 12 by 240. In arithmetic we learned that we always divide the numerator by the denominator."

"Go ahead and divide and see what you get," suggested Alberta.

Eugene scribbled on the paper and announced, "I get .05 for an answer."

"Good," said Alberta. "Can you write that as a fraction?"

"Sure," answered Eugene. ".05 = $\frac{5}{100}$, and if I reduce that I get $\frac{1}{20}$."

Alberta pounced upon his answer: "That's why you divided the flour by 20! You were calculating the amount you will need for $\frac{1}{20}$ of the original recipe."

"I get it!" Eugene wrote the following equation on the paper: $\frac{12}{240}$ = .05 = $\frac{5}{100}$ = $\frac{1}{20}$. "These are all different ways of saying the same thing."

"So," said Alberta. "We agree that we need to find one-twentieth of all these ingredients. First, take the flour. What's $\frac{1}{20}$ of 70 pounds?"

"Let's write it down," suggested Eugene, "so we can figure it out."

Alberta and Eugene sat down with a pencil and paper. "Seventy pounds divided by twenty is three and one-half pounds," Alberta said, "so we need three and one-half pounds of flour for the smaller recipe." She wrote: 70 pounds ÷ 20 = $3\frac{1}{2}$ pounds.

"Should I go to the lab and find a scale to weigh the flour?" Eugene asked.

"There's no need—we can easily measure it in cups," Alberta said. "There are about four cups of flour in a pound, and we need three and one-half pounds, so how many cups is that?"

"Well, let me see . . . three and one-half is seven halves, and seven halves times four equals 28 halves, which equals . . .14! We need 14 cups of flour."

Alberta wrote: 4 cups $\times$ $3\frac{1}{2}$ = 14 cups.

"Good," Alberta said. "Now let's figure out the rest of the ingredients."

Meanwhile, Carver checked up on Josephine. "How's the soup recipe coming?" he asked.

"Fine!" Josephine replied. "The recipe only makes enough for four people, but since we're cooking for 12, we have to triple everything. We're just measuring the flour now. I figure we need 12 tablespoons. Charles, hand me that tablespoon, will you?"

Carver raised his hand. "Hold on a minute, Josephine—it will take a long time to measure 12 tablespoons one at a time. Can you think of a faster way?"

"Well, we have larger measures, but I don't know how many tablespoons they hold," Josephine said.

"That should be easy to figure out," Carver answered. "Why don't you find out how many tablespoons it takes to fill this quarter-cup?"

"The quarter-cup holds exactly four tablespoons," Josephine said. "Now I can use it to measure the flour."

"Very good, Josephine. I'll check back again in a while to see how you're doing."

One week before the luncheon, Carver and his students met in the kitchen. "Now that we've decided on a menu," Carver said, "we need to make a schedule for the day of the cooking. We want to be sure that everything goes smoothly and that all the food is ready at the same time."

Louis thought about the various items on the menu. "We don't have to worry about the salad," he said, "because you said that you will make it yourself from greens with a peanut dressing. And we can make the coffee and crank the ice cream while the guests are eating the meal. We're going to make the soup and the candy the day before, and we will bake the bread early in the morning. That leaves the mock chicken loaf, the vegetable dish, and the cookies."

"Well, we want to serve the luncheon at 1 o'clock," said Carver. "Let's look at the recipes to find out how long each item takes to make."

Louis went down his list. "The vegetable and its creamed peanut sauce will take at least an hour to prepare and cook on the stove."

"So we'll begin that one at noon. What about the cookies?"

"The cookies take 15 minutes to bake."

"So we can start them at 12:45, right?" asked Buford.

Louis laughed. "Hold on, Buford! We had better add 5 minutes for mixing all the ingredients, and 10 minutes for shaping the cookies and putting them on the trays."

Louis added, "We also have to figure out whether to bake all the cookies at the same time or whether we'll need to do them in different batches."

"Good thinking," agreed Carver. "I have to use the oven for the mock chicken starting at noon, so we can only bake one tray of cookies at a time."

Buford figured out loud. "So if we make 3 cookies each for 12 people, that's 36 cookies, or three dozen. We can put a dozen cookies on a tray. That means we'll need three trays."

Louis was impressed. "Hey, that's really using your head, Buford! So I'll have to bake three trays of cookies, one tray at a time. If we allow 15 minutes to mix and shape the cookies and add an extra 15 minutes to be on the safe side, we should start the cookies at a quarter till twelve."

Louis was pleased with their planning. "Finally we have a schedule!"

11:45 Start making cookies.
12:00 Put mock chicken loaf in oven.
12:00 Begin creamed vegetable.

"This meal is shaping up very nicely," Carver declared. "I can't wait until Saturday to see the expressions on the faces of our guests when I tell them what they've been eating!"

"Well, I can wait!" Eugene said. "In fact, I think I'll just go wait in my room. Just let me know when it's all over."

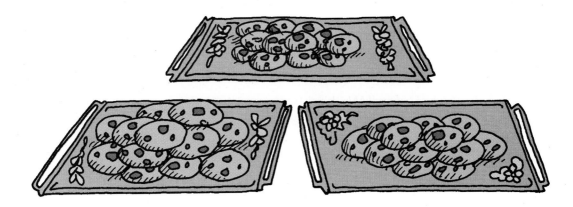

On the day of the luncheon, the kitchen was full of activity. "Clear the road! I'm coming through with the water!" Buford yelled as he entered, balancing a huge bucket of water on his head.

Eugene looked up. "Hey, Buford—that bucket looks good on your head. I think you oughta wear it to church next Sunday!"

"Oh, yeah? Well, how about if we find out how a bucket full of water looks on *your* head!"

"It wouldn't look as dumb as we're all going to look, making a dinner that has peanuts in *everything!*"

"It's not dumb!" Buford protested. "It's going to be great. Besides, Professor says that it will all taste so good, no one will even know they're eating goobers."

"Yeah, right!" Eugene laughed. "Well, I'll make you a bet. If nobody guesses that this stuff has goobers in it, I'll scrub all the pots myself."

Alberta, who had been listening to the boys' discussion, interrupted. "Eugene, please stop teasing Buford. And, Buford, what are you doing? Why are you trying to carry so much water on your head? Somebody help get that bucket down, before it—"

Just then, the water's weight proved too much for Buford. "Look out! AAArrgghhh!" He tripped, spilling water everywhere.

The students stood silently, awaiting Carver's reaction. He remained calm. "Buford, dry yourself off and meet me outside. You can help me fetch some greens for the salad. While we're gone, I'm going to depend on the rest of you to help each other and work together to make this luncheon a success. Alberta, would you please take charge?"

"Yes, sir," Alberta answered. "All right, everyone, we only have one more hour until the guests arrive. Lucy, will you please take charge of setting the table? I'm just putting the mock chicken in now. Eugene, please stop playing with those eggs, and get them cracked for the ice cream."

Buford was quick to apologize for the trouble. "I sure am sorry, Professor—I was only trying to help. I'll do better now! I'll find the best greens, and I'll carry them for you, and I'll help you wash them and toss them—these will be the best darned greens those old high-hats ever ate! These greens—"

"Buford," interrupted Carver, stooping to pick some greens, "there's no need to be disrespectful toward our guests. Some of these 'high-hats,' as you call them, are good friends of mine, and many of them have done a lot to help Tuskegee."

"Yes, sir. I'm sorry. Hey, Professor—look at all these dandelion greens! There are enough here for ten luncheons."

"Yes, but wild greens taste best when you use a variety. I'd like to find some pokeweed and some rabbit tobacco. Let's look over there. . . ."

Meanwhile, the students were getting nervous in the kitchen. "I hope Professor Carver returns soon," said Eugene as he looked out the window. "I don't see him anywhere. Those greens might be the only good part of this meal!"

Alberta looked around the kitchen. "Everything's ready! All we need are the greens. But where can Professor Carver be?"

Eugene looked out the door. "I don't know. Maybe they decided to skip this nutty lunch!"

Just then, Carver and Buford returned with their arms full of greens. "Here we are! How's it going?"

"Thank goodness you're back!" Alberta cried. "You're just in time to greet the guests!"

Buford turned to Eugene. "Quick—help me wash these greens!"

The Tuskegee luncheon was a great success. After the meal, when the guests had eaten enthusiastically and praised the cooks, Carver announced that every dish had contained peanuts.

The businessmen were amazed and asked many questions. They learned that milk and butter—even pickles—could be made from the lowly goober, as well as cheese, coffee, and many useful nonfood products. Carver explained how the peanut was an easy crop to grow and how it enriched the soil. The businessmen agreed that there might be a profitable future for the peanut.

And Eugene scrubbed all the pots.

Bats

BANDELIER NATIONAL MONUMENT FRIJOLES CANYON

CLIFF DWELLINGS OF THE ANASAZI

RUINS OF THE TYUONYI PUEBLO

BAT CAVE IN THE CLIFFS ABOVE LONG HOUSE RUINS

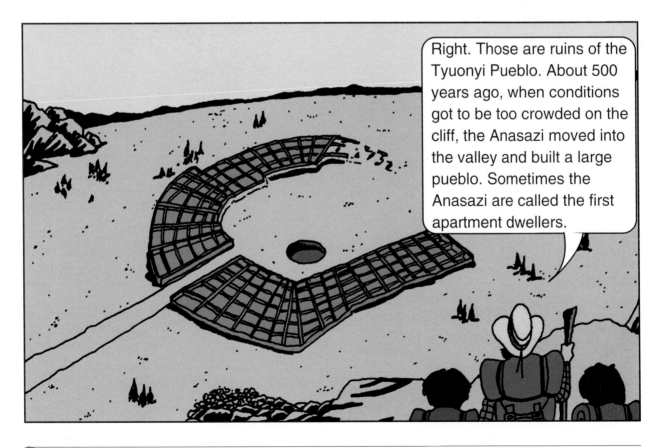

After the trap has been lowered and the bag has been removed from the trap…

Great! We caught about 100 bats. John and I will look at each one while you record the data, Sarah.

I'm ready.

This one is a female. She doesn't have a band.

That's number one. You can let her go.

John Eagle has another bat.

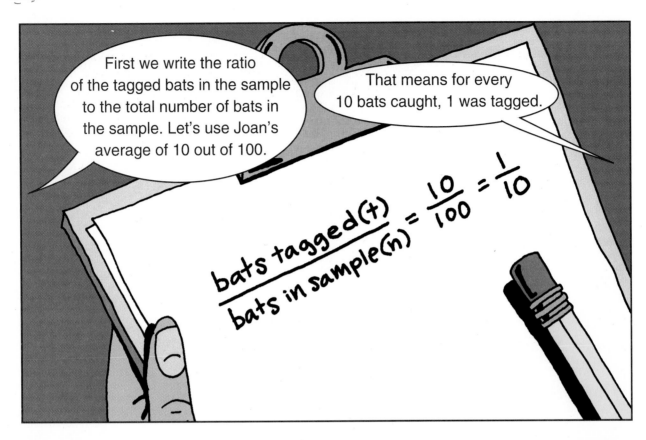

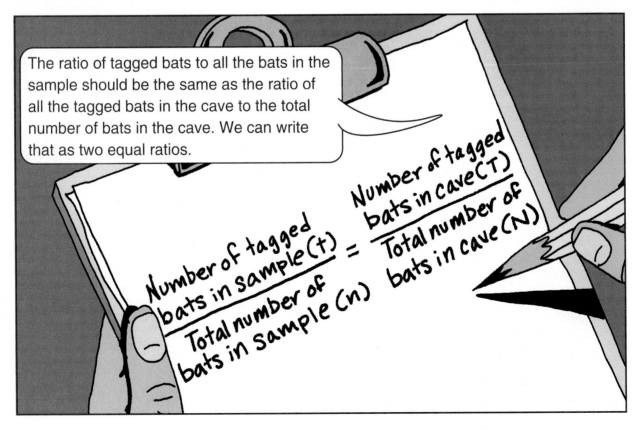

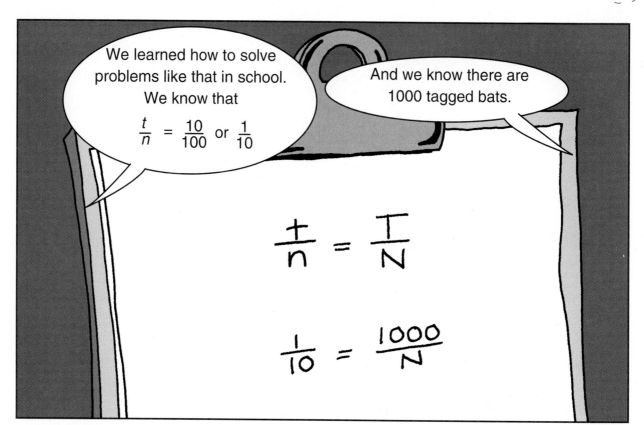